Living on the Edge
SKYDIVING

Shane McFee

PowerKiDS press.

New York

Published in 2008 by The Rosen Publishing Group, Inc.
29 East 21st Street, New York, NY 10010

First Edition

Editor: Joanne Randolph
Book Design: Kate Laczynski
Photo Researcher: Jessica Gerweck

Photo Credits: Cover, p. 1 © Joe McBride/Getty Images; pp. 4, 6, 18, 20 Shutterstock.com; p. 8 © www.istockphoto.com/Jeff McDonald; p. 10 © www.istockphoto.com/Francisco Neri; p. 14 © www.istockphoto.com/Christophe Michot; p. 12 © U.S. Government image; p. 16 © Emmler/Laif/Aurora Photos.

Library of Congress Cataloging-in-Publication Data

McFee, Shane.
    Skydiving / Shane McFee. — 1st ed.
        p. cm. — (Living on the edge)
    Includes index.
    ISBN 978-1-4042-4215-9 (library binding)
    1. Skydiving—Juvenile literature. I. Title.
    GV770.M38 2008
    797.5'6—dc22
                                                            2007033673

Manufactured in the United States of America

CONTENTS

Take a Dive

Have you ever wanted to jump out of an airplane? Does this sound like a bad idea? Three million people jump out of airplanes every year. They are called skydivers.

People all over the world enjoy skydiving. Most skydivers jump for fun. Other skydivers are good enough to **compete** in skydiving **contests**.

Skydiving is not nearly as **dangerous** as it sounds. Do you want to learn more about this **extreme sport**? This book will teach you about different types of skydiving. Maybe you will try it yourself someday.

This skydiver is coming in for a landing after a jump. Today most parachutes are rectangles, like this one, rather than the round ones you might think of.

For the Fun of It

Believe it or not, skydivers jump out of airplanes because it is fun. Skydiving gives them a **thrill**. This is the same reason people snowboard, ride roller coasters, and climb mountains.

Most skydiving centers are based in a small airport. The skydiving center needs to be at a small airport so that the sky is mostly clear. You do not want to skydive with lots of planes flying around!

Most skydiving planes are small. The pilot, or driver, takes a group of jumpers into the sky. They generally jump from about 13,000 feet (3,962 m). That is taller than most mountains. It is almost the length of 40 football fields.

This person sits on a platform, waiting to jump. For some people, the minutes before actually jumping from the airplane are the scariest of all!

Flying or Falling?

When skydivers jump, they are in freefall. Have you ever seen skydivers on television? They look like they are flying. This is not really what is happening, though. Skydivers in freefall are actually falling.

Once a skydiver gets close to the ground, he or she needs to open the parachute. Parachutes are made from special cloth. They are folded tightly and packed into a special backpack. When a parachute opens, it fills with air. The open parachute slows the skydiver down. This allows the person to land safely.

People say that freefall feels more like flying than falling. This skydiver is wearing a helmet, special clothes, and a tool that tells him how high up he is.

In It to Win

Some skydivers compete in skydiving contests. There are many different types of skydiving contests. Sometimes skydivers compete to see who can aim their parachute the best.

Skydivers also compete in freefall. Some try to freefall the fastest or the farthest.

Many master skydivers do tricks. The most popular parachute trick is called the swoop. A swoop is a very fast approach. The swooper tries to keep moving forward once the parachute is close to the ground. Swoops are very dangerous.

In one kind of skydiving competition, groups of skydivers try to create shapes during freefall. Groups can number from a few people to up to 400.

It's Not All Fun and Games

Not every skydiver jumps for fun. Some of the very first skydivers were soldiers. Soldiers who skydive are called paratroopers. The **military** often uses paratroopers to land in areas that are hard to reach. This job takes a lot of skill and bravery.

Military pilots use parachutes, too, when their plane is crashing. This is called bailing out.

Forest fires can be hard to fight in areas where there are no roads. Smoke jumpers are special firefighters who parachute in to fight fires in these hard to reach places. They carry their firefighting tools with them while they jump.

Here paratroopers land on a grassy plain during training. Paratroopers put themselves in danger every time they jump.

The Best

Master skydivers jump in lots of different ways. Some skydivers race. Some try to land as close as possible to a rocking chair. The first skydiver who sits in the chair and rocks is the winner. This is called hit and rock. Some skydivers tie a small board to their feet. This is called skysurfing.

BASE jumpers do not jump out of airplanes at all. They jump off buildings, bridges, and cliffs. BASE jumping is very dangerous because the jumpers are not that high up when they jump. They do not have much time to open their parachutes.

This person is BASE jumping off the Jin Mao Tower, in Shanghai, China. Only highly skilled skydivers should try BASE jumping.

Practice Makes Perfect

Beginning skydivers do not start by jumping out of planes. First beginning jumpers have to finish training classes. The training classes teach beginners how to jump safely.

Most skydiving centers provide **instructors**, or teachers. Instructors show beginners how to position their body in freefall. They also teach beginners how and when to open their parachutes.

Some skydiving students practice freefall in machines called wind tunnels. Wind tunnels blow powerful blasts of air, which can lift you off the ground. Beginning skydivers do not jump alone. They jump with instructors.

The beginner and the instructor usually share the same parachute, like these two jumpers are.

Safe Landings

Skydiving is safer than it seems, but it is still dangerous. Skydivers need to be very careful. Beginners must listen to their instructors.

Sometimes a parachute may fail to open. Skydivers have a backup parachute in case this happens. It is important to have an expert check both of your parachutes before you jump.

Bad parachutes are not what cause most skydiving **injuries**. Most injuries occur after the parachute has opened during the landing. The skydiver might come in too quickly or at a bad angle.

People who compete in skydiving contests must practice a lot in order to stay safe. This skydiver practices hitting a target in the center of a large mat.

Tools of the Trade

Skydivers use lots of special **equipment**. The most important tool is clearly the parachute! Some skydivers open their parachutes themselves. Many beginners have parachutes that open without help.

Skydivers also use an altimeter. Most altimeters look like wristwatches. They do not tell time, though. They tell you how high up you are. This is important. You need to know when to open your parachute!

Skydivers also wear a helmet and goggles. Skydiving helmets look like motorcycle helmets. Goggles are glasses that keep your eyes safe.

This skydiver is wearing a helmet, goggles, and a jumpsuit. The jumpsuit is meant to allow easy movement in freefall.

Living on the Edge

Does skydiving sound fun? Does it sound a little scary? Do not worry. You are likely too young to skydive today. Most skydiving centers will not allow you to jump until you are 18.

You can still learn how to skydive by practicing with instructors, though. Maybe you can even try going in a wind tunnel.

You can also **research** skydiving to learn more about the sport. You can start by looking at the United States Parachuting Association's Web site, at www.uspa.org. Skydivers live on the edge because they enjoy the thrill. Is skydiving the right sport for you?

GLOSSARY

compete (kum-PEET) To go against another in a game or test.

contests (KAHN-tests) Games in which two or more people try to win.

dangerous (DAYN-jeh-rus) Might cause hurt.

equipment (uh-KWIP-mint) All the supplies needed to do something.

extreme sport (ek-STREEM SPORT) A bold and uncommon sport, such as street luge, skateboarding, BMX, and wakeboarding.

injuries (INJ-reez) Harm or hurt done to a person's body.

instructors (in-STRUK-turz) People who teach someone how to do something.

military (MIH-lih-ter-ee) Referring to the part of the government, such as the army or navy, that keeps its citizens safe.

research (REE-serch) To study something carefully to find out more about it.

thrill (THRIL) A feeling of pleasure.

INDEX

WEB SITES

Due to the changing nature of Internet links, PowerKids Press has developed an online list of Web sites related to the subject of this book. This site is updated regularly. Please use this link to access the list:
www.powerkidslinks.com/edge/sky/